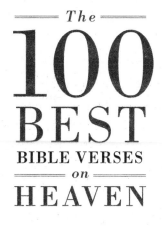

The

100

BEST

BIBLE VERSES

on

HEAVEN

Books by Troy Schmidt

The 100 Best Bible Verses on Prayer
The 100 Best Bible Verses on Heaven

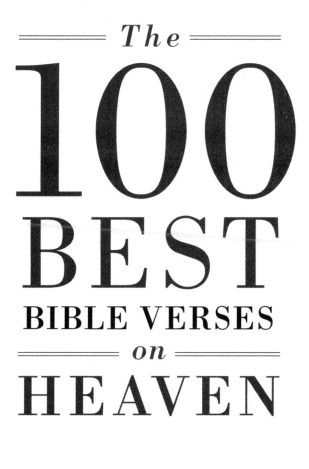

The 100 BEST BIBLE VERSES *on* HEAVEN

TROY SCHMIDT

BETHANYHOUSE

a division of Baker Publishing Group

Minneapolis, Minnesota

Published by Bethany House Publishers
11400 Hampshire Avenue South
Bloomington, Minnesota 55438
www.bethanyhouse.com

Bethany House Publishers is a division of
Baker Publishing Group, Grand Rapids, Michigan

Printed in the United States of America

Library of Congress Control Number: 2016930770

ISBN: 978-0-7642-1759-3

Cover design by Darren Welch Design LLC

The author is represented by Working Title Agency

16 17 18 19 20 21 22   7 6 5 4 3 2 1

For Santini

Who went to heaven way too soon,
but whose influence is still felt on earth today

INTRODUCTION

As a pastor, I've done my share of funerals.

And you can tell the difference between believers and non-believers.

The Christians who died and were saved by faith in Jesus Christ have way better funerals. Family and friends come together to grieve, but yet they also have hope. They know that person is in the presence of God and rejoice in their transition into heaven. They are happy for the departed and sad for themselves. They know God will heal all wounds, but it will take time. In the meantime, they celebrate their loved one's life and lasting legacy.

The funerals of the unsaved or the unsure are depressing. Nobody really understands or knows what to believe. Because they don't have faith in God, they can't be sure where the departed is at the moment or whether they will see them again.

Sad, sad, sad.

The Bible wants us to know about heaven. It's not a mystery that we'll one day discover. All the information we need to know about heaven is in the Bible. We know enough to believe, but not too much that we won't be eternally surprised.

So many times people look at heaven as a place, a paradise, a playground where we'll be free of illness and enjoying an eternal party.

Not entirely. Heaven is a relationship. That relationship happens in a place. We are there to be with God. Imagine going to Grandma's house and loving her basement and her yard and all the fun things to do there, but you ignore her.

God is what heaven will be all about. Will we enjoy the place and the people and the things to do? Sure, but none of it would be possible without the relationship with God!

Finding the one hundred best Bible verses about heaven was surprisingly easy. The information is clear and the truth refreshing. It was a joy to discover each truth; my anticipation to be there grew with each passage.

This book will explore verses about death, the afterlife, heaven, hell, and the return of Jesus Christ. Yes, it will look at the good and the bad, but to appreciate the best we need to understand the worst.

If you're like me, you'll be thinking about your loved ones who have died—some with old age, others tragically, many way too soon—but hopefully after reading these verses you'll be at peace, knowing they are truly in a better place, face-to-face with God in a wonderful relationship called heaven.

Troy Schmidt
Windermere, FL
January 2016

GENESIS 3:19

By the sweat of your face
you shall eat bread,
till you return to the ground,
for out of it you were taken;
for you are dust,
and to dust you shall return. (ESV)

L ife is hard and then you die.
That saying seems cruel, but it's how the Bible first introduces us to death and dying in Genesis 3.

We were not meant to have a hard life, but a fulfilling, eternal life. Life should come easily and naturally. Instead we have to work hours and hours every day to put food on our tables. Sin messed everything up.

And what reward do we get for all that hard work? Bodies that wear out and die.

God's pre-sin intention for our life here on earth gives us an indication about life over there in heaven, where we will no longer sweat or be exhausted and unfulfilled, but easily find what we need when we need it. No longer will we deteriorate and dissolve into dust. We will forever be eternally strong.

The Bible begins with bad news about death. It ends with good news about eternal life.

GENESIS 3:22

And the LORD God said, "The man has now become like one of us, knowing good and evil. He must not be allowed to reach out his hand and take also from the tree of life and eat, and live forever."

The Tree of Life symbolized eternal life given to us by God. The Tree of Knowledge of Good and Evil became a symbol of our pride to be like God.

Two fruits. One is ripe and sweet. The other makes us spoiled and rotten.

In the Garden, man had the choice to either hold on to eternal life or go after a selfish God-like status. Arrogantly, we turned our backs on living forever as mere humans. We wanted to attain God's knowledge of good and evil and be more like Him. For some reason, that seemed better than eternal life. We thought it would bring a richer life. We were wrong.

Before we die, we must repent of our desire to be like God (the Tree of Knowledge of Good and Evil) and accept the gift of eternal life (the Tree of Life) given to us by God. It's a decision of our will and an acknowledgment of our selfishness.

If we want to be God and run things our way, there is no room for us in heaven. There is only room for one God.

Eternal life or selfish pride? Which fruit looks tastiest to you?

GENESIS 5:24

Enoch walked faithfully with God; then he was no more, because God took him away.

Enoch got a pretty sweet deal.

After hundreds of years of faithful service, he received a private escort into the arms of God. God just took him away to heaven, to be with Him.

Today, we don't live as long as Enoch did, and though we may have been faithful our whole lives, we could still die a long, exhausting death. But it's not how you die—quick or slow—it's where you go after you die that matters.

No matter how a Christian dies, it never compares to life on the other side. A slow death with years of medical treatment on earth seems like seconds on eternity's time schedule.

Walk faithfully now and prepare for that moment when God escorts you to Him. Accept any delays as bonus time to spend with those you love.

GENESIS 25:8

Then Abraham breathed his last and died at a good old age, an old man and full of years; and he was gathered to his people.

The best way to die would be like Abraham—at a good old age and full of years.

Not just a lot of years, but years that were full of activity, blessing, and relationships.

Abraham's faithful life still impacts people today. The faces of those in this verse called "his people" grows every day.

What a perfect way to be gathered to our own people, a family reunion in heaven to talk about the past and discuss how God so richly blessed us.

Abraham lived a full life here on earth and then an even fuller life in heaven with his loved ones by his side—faces he knew and faces he continues to meet today.

Our lives on earth are counted in years. In heaven it's counted by relationships.

Make your years now be fulfilling, enriching, and impactful for your family and generations to come.

GENESIS 28:12

He had a dream in which he saw a stairway resting on the earth, with its top reaching to heaven, and the angels of God were ascending and descending on it.

There's a real stairway to heaven.

Jacob saw a stairway between heaven and earth that indicated a connection between the two very diverse places.

It's important to know those were angels, not human souls who traveled across the gap. Angels enter and exit heaven to come to earth, to perform their tasks assigned by God.

People don't.

When our loved ones leave, they are securely in a place on the other side and have no need to travel back to us.

But be comforted to know that angels are on the job surrounding us and protecting us during difficult times.

6

EXODUS 12:13

The blood shall be a sign for you, on the houses where you are. And when I see the blood, I will pass over you, and no plague will befall you to destroy you, when I strike the land of Egypt. (ESV)

On the night of the first Passover, it was the blood of the lamb on the doorposts of a home that caused death to "pass over" the people. If the people trusted the commands of God, placing the blood on their homes, they would not die.

The blood of the ceremonial lamb used in the Old Testament foreshadowed the blood of the true Lamb of God who takes away the sin of the world—Jesus Christ. Those who trust in Jesus will not die. Death will pass over their lives and allow them to enter eternal life in heaven.

Trust the blood of Jesus.

Apply it to your life.

Wave good-bye to death as it passes by.

EXODUS 15:13

"In your unfailing love you will lead
the people you have redeemed.
In your strength you will guide them
to your holy dwelling."

Every time the president travels he has an escort of Secret Service agents and police officers.

When we travel to heaven, we'll get an escort, too, guided by God to His holy dwelling.

What a reassuring idea! You thought twenty-five Secret Service agents and fifty heavily armed police officers would give you a comforting feeling of security, but they cannot compare with a regiment of angels taking you to the ultimate White House—our Father's house!

This means that no devilish plans or demonic attacks can interrupt our progress to heaven.

If God is in charge of security, we are in the best hands. We will arrive at our destination safe and sound.

EXODUS 33:19–20

> Then He said, "I will make all My goodness pass before you, and I will proclaim the name of the LORD before you. I will be gracious to whom I will be gracious, and I will have compassion on whom I will have compassion." But He said, "You cannot see My face; for no man shall see Me, and live." (NKJV)

God told Moses that nobody can see the face of God and live.

This means that seeing the face of God is such a breathtaking, awesome experience that our human bodies cannot comprehend or handle the gravity of it. Upon seeing His face, our sinful, finite bodies immediately collapse.

However, if you're already dead, then you can see His face . . . because you can't die if you're already dead.

So for eternity, in our resurrected bodies, we will constantly see the face of God and live. The experience that would kill us on earth is a wonderful daily routine in heaven. We will respond with such joy that the only thing we can possibly do is praise Him.

Praise will be our release valve for the emotions welling up inside us as we look at the face of God and express how amazing He is.

9

2 SAMUEL 12:22–23

He said, "While the child was still alive, I fasted and wept, for I said, 'Who knows whether the LORD will be gracious to me, that the child may live?' But now he is dead. Why should I fast? Can I bring him back again? I shall go to him, but he will not return to me." (ESV)

David mourned the loss of his newborn son from Bathsheba. He prayed and agonized for the child's recovery, but it was not meant to be.

When David heard the news, he switched gears and said there was nothing he could do any longer except hope for the moment when he would be reunited with his child in heaven.

What a comforting thought for those experiencing the loss of a baby. This verse seems to answer the troubling question, "Do newborns who die go to heaven?" David thought they would. He felt he would see his child—whose life-span on earth lasted only days or weeks—again in heaven. A reunion of sorts is hinted at in this verse that gives so many grieving parents hope today.

We may never get to hold those babies in our arms here on earth, but we'll get a big hug from them in heaven.

ESTHER 4:16

"Go, assemble all the Jews who are found in Susa, and fast for me; do not eat or drink for three days, night or day. I and my maidens also will fast in the same way. And thus I will go in to the king, which is not according to the law; and if I perish, I perish." (NASB)

Death did not scare Esther.

She had to do the right thing even if it meant the king took her life.

Perishing is not the worst thing that can happen to us in this lifetime.

The worst thing would be preserving our own life while others died.

You don't want to end your life full of regrets and what-ifs. Or look back and not see a hint of sacrifice.

Don't fear death, which takes away your life on earth. Fear selfishness, which takes away a true and meaningful life that can impact both heaven and earth.

Do what God directs you to do . . . and if you die . . . you die. . . .

What's the worst that can happen?

JOB 1:21

And he said:
"Naked I came from my mother's womb,
And naked shall I return there.
The LORD gave, and the LORD has taken away;
Blessed be the name of the LORD." (NKJV)

No one is born wearing a sequined gown or a tuxedo. We all arrive naked into the world. The same dress code.

Later in life, depending on our family and social status, some of us dress in the finest Gucci clothes while others get hand-me-downs from Goodwill.

Then, as life begins to wind down, we all share one thing in common again. We all leave the same way we came. Our souls depart this earth with nothing in hand. Name brands make no difference. Rich and poor get the same treatment.

Death.

We all have a naked birth-day and a naked death-day; it's how we live the days in between that makes us unique.

God gives life and takes away life. But, like Job, we should praise Him for whatever clothes we get to wear and for every opportunity He gives us on this earth.

JOB 13:15

"Though he slay me, yet will I hope in him;
I will surely defend my ways to his face."

Can we really have hope in our slayer?
Job thought so. He felt that even if God ended his life right then, he would still have hope.

Job even felt confident facing his slayer because he had led a righteous life. We should live knowing that someday we will face our Maker and have to answer for our choices.

Are you prepared to defend your life? Excuses won't work. Alibis wear thin. Our only hope is knowing that Jesus Christ died for all our sins. Our sins are all paid for. Job didn't have that hope in Jesus Christ; he didn't know about Him. Yet Job trusted that God would take care of him someday . . . somehow . . . and He did.

For us, we know more than Job, so our hope is more secure.

Death was not the end of hope for Job. Death confirmed the hope he had.

3

JOB 14:5

A person's days are determined;
you have decreed the number of his months
and have set limits he cannot exceed.

God has already determined the number of days we will live on this earth.

And aren't we glad He has kept this a secret from us? We need to live every day as if it were our last.

Whether it's a short life or a long life, God knows best.

Every month matters. Every day matters. For that matter, so does every hour, minute, and second.

Our time is set and cannot be shortened or lengthened. There's nothing we can do but accept it.

Our death does not take God by surprise, and it shouldn't surprise us, either. We know that when that day arrives, God, in His wisdom, has determined it so.

JOB 19:25–27

For I know that my Redeemer lives,
and at the last he will stand upon the earth.
And after my skin has been thus destroyed,
yet in my flesh I shall see God,
whom I shall see for myself,
and my eyes shall behold, and not another.
My heart faints within me! (ESV)

Our Redeemer lives and we will see Him face-to-face.
Even Job, whose book some think is the oldest in
the Bible, believed in a resurrection and an afterlife. He
knew he would see God after his death (his skin destroyed) and
during his own resurrection (in his own flesh). He looked forward to the moment when he would see God with his own eyes.

Can any other sight be more magnificent than that? Throughout the Bible, people awaited that incredible moment.

You and your loved ones will see God in fully resurrected
bodies.

Just wait and see . . . with your own eyes!

JOB 33:28

"God has delivered me from going down to the pit,
and I shall live to enjoy the light of life."

G od loves to rescue people from the pits—literally. Joseph was in a pit, then went to prison, then rose to be Pharaoh's right-hand man.

Daniel was in a pit with lions, then also rose to be the king's trusted advisor.

God has rescued us from the pits, too—the pits of hell—and we will one day rise to be by His side.

We were once banished and left to die because of our sins. Then, because of what Jesus did on the cross, we rose to be heirs with the King of Kings.

It's a dark place in those pits, but God pulls us out to see the light . . . the eternal light of heaven.

PSALM 14:2

The LORD has looked down from heaven upon the
  sons of men
To see if there are any who understand,
Who seek after God. (NASB)

Imagine God's perspective of us from heaven, looking down
and thinking, *If you could only see things from here.*

From our vantage point we don't understand. From God's
vantage point we would.

We can't fathom the vastness of this earth until we're on a
plane. We don't understand the power of a city until we're on
the top floor of a skyscraper.

Those in heaven now understand. They see why they needed
to die. They see why earth is so messed up. They see the big
picture.

As we mourn the loss of loved ones, seek to see things from
God's perspective. From heaven, the view is much clearer.

PSALM 16:9–10

Therefore my heart is glad and my tongue rejoices;
my body also will rest secure,
because you will not abandon me to the realm of the
dead,
nor will you let your faithful one see decay.

This verse, though applied directly to Jesus by Peter in Acts 2, applies to all believers who have passed on and will take part in a future resurrection.

Because Jesus led the way, believers will not be abandoned in their graves.

God will not allow our lives to decay into a pile of ashes. He will resurrect the faithful in the same exact manner as He resurrected Jesus.

That is good news and should make us glad. Eternal life with God will not be about decay. It will be about growth and understanding and fulfillment, all of them the opposite of decay.

Rejoice, your life is not winding down. It's just getting started.

PSALM 18:4–6

The cords of death entangled me;
the torrents of destruction overwhelmed me.
The cords of the grave coiled around me;
the snares of death confronted me.
In my distress I called to the LORD;
I cried to my God for help.
From his temple he heard my voice;
my cry came before him, into his ears.

As death wraps itself around us—whether slowly or quickly—we can cry out to God for help.

Like the ultimate lifeguard, God hears us as the torrents of death splash over us and the currents pull us down to the depths.

As long as God is watching over us, we cannot drown in our graves.

But we have to cry out first, while there is still time, letting God know that we trust Him to save us.

By doing so, we acknowledge that God and only God can save us. His ears perk up. His attention turns to us. He knows we're drowning and He's ready to dive in and save us.

Just cry out.

PSALM 23:4

Yea, though I walk through the valley of the shadow
  of death,
I will fear no evil;
For You are with me;
Your rod and Your staff, they comfort me. (NKJV)

L ife's paths take us to mountain-high experiences and to
  low valley doldrums. On earth, those lowest places—
  Death Valley and the Dead Sea—get names we associate
with death.

Some valleys of life are so deep, there seems to be no way out.
With death, there is no way out. We must all walk through it.

This verse doesn't promise that we won't walk through the
dark valley of death. However, it does promise that we won't
be alone.

God has all the weapons He needs to ward off evil and get
us to the other side.

Rods to keep back the enemies of truth. Staffs to scare off
the lions of lies.

Keep on walking and experience comfort while you enter
this dark valley. God promises to bring us out to the other side.

You're not alone, and God is packing heat.

PSALM 23:6

Surely goodness and mercy shall follow me
All the days of my life;
And I will dwell in the house of the LORD
Forever. (NKJV)

How long have you been at your current address?
It may seem like forever, but it's not.
We won't truly understand forever until we move to our heavenly address.

And all that goodness and love God showed you here at this address on earth . . . it will follow you right up to heaven and make its home with you.

Every neighbor will be family, filled with nothing but more goodness and love.

That's an address to get excited about.

It will be your permanent home.

PSALM 27:4

One thing have I asked of the LORD,
   that will I seek after:
that I may dwell in the house of the LORD
   all the days of my life,
to gaze upon the beauty of the LORD
   and to inquire in his temple. (ESV)

Have you ever seen the Grand Canyon? You don't just take a quick glance at it and then walk away. You look at it, then you look at it some more, then you keep looking at it, trying to wrap your mind around it.

Gazing at God in heaven will be the same experience. We'll see Him, then look at Him again, then catch ourselves staring at Him—His power, His majesty, His beauty—over and over and over and over. . . .

This will take up much of our time in eternity as we keep gazing at God and thinking, *Wow, He looks different than He did a few minutes ago*, or, *I never saw that side of Him before.* . . .

Notice that David asked for only one thing while in heaven. He didn't ask to be with a deceased family member or his family pet or a good friend. All David asked for was to gaze at God.

In heaven, it's okay to stare. God won't mind. Fix your eyes on what heaven is all about.

PSALM 39:4–5

Show me, LORD, my life's end
and the number of my days;
let me know how fleeting my life is.
You have made my days a mere handbreadth;
the span of my years is as nothing before you.
Everyone is but a breath,
even those who seem secure.

God likes to remind us how short life is. Primarily at funerals.

It may be the death of an old person or someone who died young—way before, as we say, "their time."

But our time is not "our" time. It's God's time, and at whatever age someone dies—whether long-lived or short-lived—God makes the determination.

Time is short no matter how long someone lived. Five years or ninety-five years of life are merely a breath in light of eternity.

We need to see that reminder of death so we do not place too much importance on life here, but focus on life over there, with God in heaven, making sure we'll be there forever.

On earth, life is short. In heaven, it's eternal and only one short breath away.

23

PSALM 44:25–26

For our soul has sunk down into the dust;
Our body cleaves to the earth.
Rise up, be our help,
And redeem us for the sake of Your lovingkindness. (NASB)

W hoever thought dust could be our enemy?
Dust is a prison for our bodies, a place where our frame deteriorates and blows away after years of exposure to the elements.

But God offers to rescue us from the dust, and by His unfailing love displayed through Jesus Christ, we will rise from the graves and be freed of death.

Dust may be an annoyance around your house or cause you to sneeze, but that's the extent of its threat to any believer.

Resurrection defeats the dust. Our bodies will rise from it again.

PSALM 49:15

But God will redeem me from the realm of the dead;
he will surely take me to himself.

You gotta love those Rambo movies, when he would storm the enemy camps, find the POWs or the innocent victims locked in cages, then free them, taking out the perpetrators and destroying the camp. And because it looks cool, Rambo even throws a child over his shoulder and blasts his way out.

God has done the same thing, only this time Rambo is Jesus Christ.

Jesus Christ died and stormed the camp of death, releasing its hold, kicking open the cages, knocking out its power, then freeing all those stuck in graves.

Jesus then throws all believers over His shoulder and takes them to be with himself.

Jesus Christ is the original action hero. He has saved you from the prison and released you from the enemy.

PSALM 49:16–17

Be not afraid when a man becomes rich,
when the glory of his house increases.
For when he dies he will carry nothing away;
his glory will not go down after him. (ESV)

If a fire struck your house, what would you run in and save? Many things come to mind—pictures, computers, jewelry, maybe the cat.

But when death strikes your life, there is no last-minute scramble to grab anything.

You can't take anything with you. Those things that once mattered so much stay right here where you left them.

We put so much time and energy into things we will eventually leave behind, things that will likely get thrown into the trash.

Maybe we should put our energy into things that won't pass away but could go with us.

Like people. Their souls can travel with us to heaven. You can take people with you.

Time to start packing.

Spend time with those who matter.

PSALM 62:1–2

Truly my soul finds rest in God;
my salvation comes from him.
Truly he is my rock and my salvation;
he is my fortress, I will never be shaken.

Rest. The concept seems so foreign to us.
How do we rest in a world so troubled, so unpredictable?
Our souls will find true rest when they unite with God.
In heaven there are no troubles, no setbacks, no time crunches,
no unpredictable glitches.

Our salvation will save us from all those things.

Resting in Him will be like resting inside the most powerful
fortress ever created. No enemy can get in. No weather event
can topple it.

Our rest will be rock solid and unshakeable.

PSALM 68:20

Our God is a God who saves;
from the Sovereign LORD comes escape from death.

We like to save money by clipping coupons, watching for sales, and standing in line on Black Friday.
We like to save time by cutting corners, multitasking, and texting while driving. (Don't do it!)

We have a God who likes to save, also. He saves people. He loves doing it. It's what He does.

By saving us, He shows us that He cares about us.

By saving us, He shows us that He has power over the elements that try to defeat us.

By saving us, He shows us that He has a reason to keep us around forever.

He saves us from death and takes us to the safety of heaven, so we no longer need to fear.

So allow God to save you. He doesn't need money or time (He owns all of it).

And when you die, He'll give you everything you've been trying to save on earth—all the riches of heaven and eternity.

Quite a savings plan.

PSALM 73:25

Whom have I in heaven but You?
And besides You, I desire nothing on earth. (NASB)

Where is our true inheritance? Here on earth?
We actually have nothing here. Everything we need is in heaven.

Our inheritance is God—our relationship with Him, our time with Him, our salvation through Him.

So why would we want to stay on this earth and remain with nothing when our death allows us to have everything?

Nobody wants nothing. Everybody wants everything.

In heaven we get it all, and nothing will be held back.

PSALM 73:26

My flesh and my heart fail;
But God is the strength of my heart and my portion
   forever. (NKJV)

C ancer eats our flesh.
      Hearts get diseased and clogged, giving up, unable
to pump another beat.
These poor bodies are destined to expire.

But God will make our hearts beat once again. It will be a spiritual heart made of resurrected flesh that will pump so strongly, it lasts forever.

Which heart are we most concerned about: our physical heart or our spiritual heart? We ask doctors to check our heartbeat and blood pressure. Shouldn't we ask God to check our heart for Him and our heart for others?

If we have a heart for God, He'll one day give us a heart that will never fail. If it starts to beat for Him now, it will beat for Him eternally.

PSALM 84:10

Better is one day in your courts
than a thousand elsewhere. . . .

What's your idea of a perfect day? The beach? Relaxing on a deck in the mountains? Playing with family? A cruise?

How about a thousand consecutive days of vacationing? How does that sound?

At first it sounds great, but it will probably get boring. Another day of sand. That sun getting hot. Those birds are getting on my nerves. And those kids!

How about one day in the presence of God? Does that sound appealing? For one day you get to stare at the face of God, exploring His beauty, feeling His power, studying His complexity, relaxing in His presence, and celebrating His holiness.

How about a thousand of those days? How about an eternity?

We will never find the perfect vacation here on earth, no matter how long our break might last. That perfect retreat with the best view will only be found in heaven.

PSALM 89:47–48

Remember how fleeting is my life.
For what futility you have created all humanity!
Who can live and not see death,
or who can escape the power of the grave?

The answer to this Scripture's question is NO ONE.
No one can avoid death, nor can they escape the power of the grave.

Okay, well, one. Jesus Christ avoided the longevity of death and the power of the grave that wanted to swallow Him in and trap Him there.

Our lives on the earth may be fleeting and futile, but with Christ, our lives have meaning and purpose.

He promises to take us with Him in the resurrection. We, too, will live with Him and say good-bye to death.

So let's ask the question again: Who can live and not see death, or who can escape the power of the grave?

Answer: All those who believe in Jesus Christ.

PSALM 90:12

So teach us to number our days
that we may get a heart of wisdom. (ESV)

A wise person knows he will die.
A fool doesn't think he'll die, or he simply chooses
to ignore his mortality.
A wise person counts the days.
A fool loses track of his age and tries to turn back the clock
by acting immature.

Funerals are great places to learn wisdom. At a funeral we
are reminded of our mortality.

A wise person leaves a funeral changed, promising to live a
fuller, richer life.

A fool returns to his old ways.

Allow the reality of death to make you wiser.

PSALM 100:4

Enter into His gates with thanksgiving,
And into His courts with praise.
Be thankful to Him, and bless His name. (NKJV)

Imagine that moment when you walk into heaven . . .
As you pass by the gates and the angels standing guard, you immediately enter the courtyard. It's huge. Gigantic! It has to contain all of God in one place.

So how will you react? Hands in your pockets, nodding your head. "Impressive."

Hardly. We'll run into that courtyard like a kid entering Disney World, screaming and cheering as we experience the greatest moment of our lives.

This verse uses "thanks" twice and "praise" twice, so we'll be doubling up on the praise and thanking God that we can be there.

This is not a casual, just-passing-by moment. Entering the presence of God will cause all of our love to come pouring out. We will be so thankful that we never have to leave!

PSALM 103:14–16

. . . for he knows how we are formed,
he remembers that we are dust.
The life of mortals is like grass,
they flourish like a flower of the field;
the wind blows over it and it is gone,
and its place remembers it no more.

God knows.
He knows how we were formed. He was there. He picked up the dust and blew life into it.

He knows that things can flourish for a while, then all of a sudden . . . drought.

He knows that the winds of change blow mercilessly over our lives and alter the direction we thought we were taking.

God knows how fragile our bodies are—how quickly things can change and how forces out there can bring us down. So He responds to us with mercy.

God has an answer for our fragility—a place that will not deteriorate or turn to dust or be forgotten forever. It's a place where we'll grow like grass and flourish like flowers.

Heaven is God's answer to death.

He knows what we need.

PSALM 116:3–4

The cords of death entangled me,
the anguish of the grave came over me;
I was overcome by distress and sorrow.
Then I called on the name of the LORD:
"LORD, save me!"

The only way to be saved when drowning is to call out for help. "Save me!"

The only way to be saved from death is to call out for help. "Save me!"

However, that call cannot be to a person inexperienced at overcoming death, or any imaginary self-help fad that is now popular. That cry for help must go to the only one qualified to save us from death. The Lord.

So you must call His name so He knows you believe that He can save you.

To all those who cry "Lord, save me!" He promises to save them.

If you don't, then you must think you can save yourself. Good luck with that.

PSALM 139:16

Your eyes saw my unformed body;
  all the days ordained for me were written
    in your book
  before one of them came to be.

Apparently there's a book written about you in heaven. It details when you arrived on the scene and when you will depart. God wrote about you a long time ago.

Be thrilled to know that God wrote your story, and here you are living out that novel.

If you accept that God wrote your story, then you must accept when He writes "The end." He is the beginning and the end. He writes all our beginnings and all our ends.

Like a play, your story begins. God knows your character better than anyone and creates all the laughter and drama that you encounter. Then, when it's over, you must step down, take a bow, and thank God for all the time He gave you on life's stage.

God's a great storyteller and every day is a new chapter. Make sure you give an incredible performance.

ECCLESIASTES 3:1–2

To everything there is a season,
A time for every purpose under heaven:
A time to be born,
And a time to die;
A time to plant,
And a time to pluck what is planted. (NKJV)

It's time.

Everything in this world operates under a time schedule. That was not God's original plan. Time was supposed to equal eternity (timelessness). However, sin put an end to "forever" on this earth, and shifted "forever" to the unseen spiritual realm. "Temporary" is the new clock for earth.

So this earth and our lives live under the clock. Every second ticks closer to its expiration.

We may not like the time frame but we must accept it. There's nothing we can do.

In addition to that time to be born and that time to die, God adds a new time—a time to resurrect. That we do have control over, by accepting Jesus Christ as our Lord and Savior.

Do you believe that incredible truth?

It's time.

ECCLESIASTES 3:19–20

For what happens to the children of man and what happens
to the beasts is the same; as one dies, so dies the other. They
all have the same breath, and man has no advantage over the
beasts, for all is vanity. All go to one place. All are from the
dust, and to dust all return. (ESV)

Death has a way of equalizing us and bringing perspective to our situation.

We have the same fate as animals—we breathe the same air, then we all turn to dust.

We are no different than roadkill.

However, we have a lot more to be thankful for than a dead raccoon on the side of the road. God never promised eternal life to any animal. God never died for any animal on the cross. God never expressed His eternal love to any animal.

God loves animals and even gave them a place on the ark, but He never showed any signs of wanting them in a relationship with Him in heaven forever.

So our fates on this earth are the same as animals; however, our fates in heaven are different. God loves human beings far more.

ISAIAH 6:5

Then I said, "Woe is me, for I am ruined! Because I
am a man of unclean lips,
And I live among a people of unclean lips; For my
eyes have seen the King, the Lord of hosts." (NASB)

That moment when we first see God will not be like when
we first saw the love of our life or our firstborn child or
the moment that child graduates or gets married. Great
moments, but nothing like when we see God.

If we take our cues from Isaiah, our first reaction will be
"AHHH! I'm falling apart . . . I can't stand myself . . . This is
tearing me to pieces!"

The sight of God will be so incomprehensible that everything we ever thought or imagined will collapse. Everything we
believed was important shatters before us. We will feel useless,
dirty and insignificant, overwhelmed and overjoyed.

Then God will speak to us and comfort us, and over time
we will realize this awesome God knows us, cares for us, and
embraces us. We may never get over the awe of His presence
and constantly be catching our breaths for eternity.

ISAIAH 11:6

And the wolf will dwell with the lamb,
And the leopard will lie down with the young goat,
And the calf and the young lion and the fatling together;
And a little boy will lead them. (NASB)

Heaven is about peace.
On earth, wolves eat lambs. Leopards eat goats. Lions eat calves and yearlings.

And children need to stay away from these man-eating beasts or they'll get eaten, too.

Yet in heaven there is no killing, no survival of the fittest. The innocent are safe. All the enemies are gone and the reason for their disagreement no longer matters.

We no longer have to kill to survive in heaven. We'll need only faith to survive.

In heaven, enemies will be friends, and we'll all hang out like we were kids again.

Even the wolves won't bother the lambs, and the goats will be taking naps with leopards.

Death no longer exists in heaven. Only life and peace.

ISAIAH 38:5

"Go and say to Hezekiah, Thus says the LORD, the God of David your father: I have heard your prayer; I have seen your tears. Behold, I will add fifteen years to your life." (ESV)

If God allows it, He can add years to our lives.

This is not to say that everyone who prays will get more time, but in some cases, like Hezekiah, we can.

Unfortunately, Hezekiah made a huge mistake in those extra fifteen years. He showed off the treasures of the temple to a group from Babylon, and later those Babylonians came back to pillage and take those items away.

It's not getting more years to live that matters, it's how we live those years that makes a difference.

Sometimes it may be better that God takes us away when He originally planned so we don't make a mistake that costs so many lives.

ISAIAH 43:25

"I, I am he
who blots out your transgressions for my own sake,
and I will not remember your sins." (ESV)

In heaven, God doesn't remind you of your sins.
"Remember when you messed up big-time and caused your family all that grief?" Doesn't happen.

God erases all records of any transgressions that we ever committed. It's stricken from the archives. Erased from the computer banks. The files are permanently deleted.

But if God has forgiven us now, why do we keep searching the trash can and pulling out the deleted files? We look over those old memories and they bring up new thoughts—*God will never forgive me. I'm too unclean to be forgiven. He must hate me.*

No matter what the past says, God has forgiven you now and in the future as well.

ISAIAH 65:17

"See, I will create
new heavens and a new earth.
The former things will not be remembered,
nor will they come to mind."

We always worry about dying and leaving this world behind. All those things that were so familiar and comfortable on this earth, we hate to think that we would have to live without them.

But the beauty and amazement of the new heaven and new earth will immediately overwhelm the comfort and tradition of this old world and make it useless and irrelevant in our memory.

We will see our current situation as poverty compared to the richness of heaven, even if we live in million-dollar mansions and penthouse suites today.

So quickly will those things of this world exit our minds and never return to our conscious thoughts. We will realize that heaven offers what we've always truly wanted but could never fully find on earth.

DANIEL 6:26–27

For He is the living God and enduring forever,
And His kingdom is one which will not be destroyed,
And His dominion will be forever.
"He delivers and rescues and performs signs and wonders
In heaven and on earth. . . ." (NASB)

God's kingdom is not going anywhere. It's going to be around forever.

This earth is His kingdom. Heaven is His kingdom. When we die, we simply move from one part of His kingdom to another.

In both places, He performs signs and wonders—miraculous feats and healings. God amazes us wherever we go.

He saves us while we are on His earthly kingdom, then transports us to ultimate safety in His heavenly kingdom.

We enjoy some benefits of His kingdom while on earth, but we get every benefit as we enter heaven.

It's good to be a resident of God's kingdom. Make Him your King on earth and He'll be your King in heaven.

HOSEA 13:14

"I will deliver this people from the power of the grave;
I will redeem them from death.
Where, O death, are your plagues?
Where, O grave, is your destruction?"

This verse in Hosea was so good, Paul repeated it in 1 Corinthians 15.

The grave has power, but it doesn't have the final say. The grave destroys, but not beyond what God can repair.

Jesus Christ paid the price to get us out of death. He walked out of the grave, mocking its so-called authority.

Once thought to be so cruel, death was revealed to be a mere pussycat up against the Lion of Judah.

Grave . . . you have no power or plague, no sting or destruction. It cannot stand up against the giver of life.

JONAH 2:6

To the roots of the mountains I sank down;
the earth beneath barred me in forever.
But you, LORD my God,
brought my life up from the pit.

J onah was at the lowest point in his life.
Caught running from God, then thrown into a sea to calm the storm and protect a ship's crew, God saved Jonah by having a fish swallow him. Definition of a bad day . . .

There inside the guts of a stinky fish, with no daylight or hope in sight, Jonah praised God and confirmed His salvation. He knew God would pull him out of this pit.

Over seven hundred years later, Jesus compared Jonah's three-day adventure in a fish to Jesus' three-day stop in the grave. Both swallow people up, trapping them inside. Both places smell like death. Once there, you can't get any lower.

Both Jonah and Jesus knew God would not leave them there in the pit. God rips open the mouths of pits and pulls His people from them.

God promises that everyone who believes, like Jonah, will not remain in the grave. Next stop, resurrection and life everlasting. God takes you from the lowest point in your earthly life and elevates you to the greatest moment of your eternal life.

MATTHEW 6:19–21

Do not store up for yourselves treasures on earth, where moth and rust destroy, and where thieves break in and steal. But store up for yourselves treasures in heaven, where neither moth nor rust destroys, and where thieves do not break in or steal; for where your treasure is, there your heart will be also. (NASB)

Heaven is a safe-deposit box where we can now begin to store our stuff.

However, heaven doesn't take cash, gold, or precious-jewel deposits. We do not take any of those things with us.

What is stored in heaven? People.

People are the richest commodity that are spiritually transmitted to our accounts in heaven. When we get there and see all the people who are there because of our lives and testimonies, then we will be richly blessed. We will feel like the richest people in the world.

The bank is open and the records are being kept. Are you making a deposit there today?

MATTHEW 12:36–37

"But I tell you that every careless word that people speak, they shall give an accounting for it in the day of judgment. For by your words you will be justified, and by your words you will be condemned." (NASB)

On the day of judgment, we have to give an account for everything we did on earth, including every word we spoke. Every word.

Our words seem to be the best evidence to reveal the real us.

Our words show if we lived a life that was meaningful or empty. Guilty or free.

I can't remember things I said yesterday, but at my time of judgment every word will scroll by. I will be shocked by how many sarcastic comments I made, how many stupid responses I said, and how many vain times I used God's name.

I'd better install a filter now in my mouth to make sure that day of judgment goes much more smoothly.

MATTHEW 13:41–43

The Son of Man will send out his angels, and they will weed out of his kingdom everything that causes sin and all who do evil. They will throw them into the blazing furnace, where there will be weeping and gnashing of teeth. Then the righteous will shine like the sun in the kingdom of their Father. Whoever has ears, let them hear.

Fire is the ultimate destruction on earth. Once something turns to ashes, it loses all its power and value. You can't remake it or glue it back together.

God will one day throw everything that caused sin and all who did evil into the blazing furnace called hell. Once there, they will lose any influence and any value they may have had on earth.

Those who are there will cry for what was lost and worry over what might have been.

The righteous—those who are in a right relationship with God through Jesus Christ—will not be covered in ash and soot, but shine like the sun, completely clean, totally holy, and smiling with joy.

That's the place to be.

MATTHEW 19:28–30

Jesus said to them, "Truly, I say to you, in the new world, when the Son of Man will sit on his glorious throne, you who have followed me will also sit on twelve thrones, judging the twelve tribes of Israel. And everyone who has left houses or brothers or sisters or father or mother or children or lands, for my name's sake, will receive a hundredfold and will inherit eternal life. But many who are first will be last, and the last first." (ESV)

If you are willing to say that you would leave your home, your family, or your job for Jesus Christ, then it's obvious you have made Him the top priority of your life.

However, leaving those things would cause a deficit in your life. If you leave your job, you would have a deficit of money. If you leave behind your family, then you have less family. If you walked out of your home, you would be homeless. So where's the multiplied benefit?

Jesus promises a benefit multiplied by one hundred that would manifest itself in some ways while on earth (a greater sense of purpose, worth, or value in our belief).

But the real benefit occurs at the "renewal of all things"— when heaven opens up for the resurrected believers.

Those who sacrificed themselves on earth, willing to live with a deficit, will receive the full benefits package in heaven. Your sacrifice will pay off a hundred times over because you know where your real home will be.

MATTHEW 22:30

For in the resurrection they neither marry nor are given in marriage, but are like angels of God in heaven. (NKJV)

There is no marriage in heaven because there is no need for it.

Marriage on earth is a symbol of the intimate relationship we have with the God of heaven. When we die, we (the bride) arrive at God's (the groom's) house. We are carried across the threshold of death and to a place where we will be loved, protected, and provided for throughout eternity.

That will be our primary relationship. We may know many people in heaven, but we won't be connected to them the same way. Our relationships will be familiar, but they won't be similar to the way they were on earth.

We will be eternally focused on God, serving Him, praising Him, and connecting with His heart. He will be the only relationship we need.

MATTHEW 25:21

His lord said to him, "Well done, good and faithful servant; you were faithful over a few things, I will make you ruler over many things. Enter into the joy of your lord." (NKJV)

Academy Awards. Golden Globes. Grammys. Emmys. Medals of Freedom. Medals of Honor. Those are some pretty great awards. Well deserved.

But can you imagine any greater award than to hear God say this verse to you as you enter heaven?

You will die and leave behind the thirty-year medals and fifty-year pocket watches from your jobs. The plaques and statues will collect dust on your mantle. What will really matter when you die?

How about God paying you a compliment of appreciation for serving Him faithfully on earth . . . how would that stack up to any earthly award you've received?

It will be all the congratulations you need, and the excitement for receiving it will tickle you for eternity.

53

MATTHEW 25:31–32

When the Son of Man comes in His glory, and all the holy
angels with Him, then He will sit on the throne of His glory.
All the nations will be gathered before Him, and He will
separate them one from another, as a shepherd divides his
sheep from the goats. (NKJV)

As soon as Jesus calls it quits for the earth and establishes
a new heaven and new earth, He will plop down on His
throne and gather all the nations before Him.

There will be a seating assignment. But it's pretty simple.
Either you sit on the left or on the right.

It won't be by last name or height or denomination or in-
come. It will be by faith.

Those who believed in Jesus Christ over here. Those who
did not believe in Jesus Christ over there. Pretty simple, yet
devastatingly hard.

In heaven, it's one or the other. You either believe or you
don't. Nothing else will matter. That's when the final separation begins. And there's no turning back then.

Get your seat assignment now.

MATTHEW 25:34

"Then the King will say to those on His right, 'Come, you who are blessed of My Father, inherit the kingdom prepared for you from the foundation of the world.'" (NASB)

You want to be on the right side of God.

Those who are in a right relationship with God through Jesus Christ will get an inheritance, a kingdom that has been waiting for them since God created the world. It will be pristine and perfect.

It will be . . . just right.

Belief in God and a righteous relationship with God get you into heaven.

So get it right now and be in the right when you arrive before God and His throne and take a seat on the right.

It's the right place to be for eternity.

MATTHEW 25:46

These will go away into eternal punishment, but the righteous into eternal life. (NASB)

A crossroads. A really important crossroads. One group goes one way and one group goes the other. Never to see the other again.

The sign at the crossroads points to two completely opposite directions. You can't get more different. They are as far apart as the north is from the south.

It will come down to one or the other. Black and white, no gray area.

But the choice won't occur at the crossroads. The choice occurred over the person's life-span. At some point he or she made decisions to go left or right—with God or away from God. Then they will die and go where their choice takes them.

Punishment or life . . . what about you? Which do you choose? Know where you're going before you hit the road.

MARK 12:27

He is not the God of the dead, but of the living; you are
greatly mistaken. (NASB)

In this statement, Jesus is saying that God does not rule over
the dead but the living.

Why? The dead don't want God. They are "dead" to Him
and any thought of Him. That's why they are dead. They have
refused the giver of life.

The living live because they recognize where true life is
found—in Jesus Christ, the Way, the Truth, and the Life.

God does not rule over death. In Revelation, death and the
grave are tossed away, never to be a threat again. Death means
sin, and that's not God.

That means that those who are dead but who have Christ
are really alive, because they are God's and will never lose their
life again.

That's life!

Go on living.

LUKE 16:22–23

The time came when the beggar died and the angels carried him to Abraham's side. The rich man also died and was buried. In Hades, where he was in torment, he looked up and saw Abraham far away, with Lazarus by his side.

To be far from God is torment.

The rich man, during this one moment, saw the kind of relationship Lazarus had with Abraham. Close. Loving. The beggar got a personal escort to his eternal resting place by angels. He was taken to be with one of the Bible's greatest heroes—a patriarch even, a superstar of the Old Testament. The beggar was being comforted, cared for, and protected, all the things the rich man was not experiencing in hell.

It's good to see the kind of experience our loved ones will have in heaven. In heaven, it's all about relationship and finding comfort and love.

As for those in hell, it's about separation—no one to help, no way out, all alone. In hell, the rich become beggars, crying out for relationship.

LUKE 16:26

"And besides all this, between us and you a great chasm has been fixed, in order that those who would pass from here to you may not be able, and none may cross from there to us." (ESV)

In the story of the beggar and the rich man, Abraham told the rich man that between heaven and hell is a great divide with no possible way for either to cross over to the other.

We have only one shot here on earth to get it right in heaven. No appeal process. No classes where we learn how to get our lives right. No late night bridge crossings, sneaking over to the other side.

If we did get a second chance, we would blow off the first chance and do what we wanted, always knowing in the back of our minds that we could slip in later. Sorry, no loopholes in the afterlife.

Don't find yourself on the wrong side of the chasm. Choose to be on God's side now and He'll guarantee that you are there forever.

LUKE 16:27–28

"He answered, 'Then I beg you, father, send Lazarus to my family, for I have five brothers. Let him warn them, so that they will not also come to this place of torment.'"

Jesus continued telling the story about the exchange between Abraham, Lazarus, and the rich man: The rich man, realizing his place in hell was locked, decided to plea for his family to enter heaven. He knew their situation and their hearts, and if things didn't change for them quickly, they, too, would end up like him.

So the rich man asked that someone send them a warning. Abraham said that Moses and the prophets had given plenty of warnings in their writings. The rich man countered, "Maybe someone from the dead." Abraham shook his head. If the Scriptures weren't enough, a ghost wouldn't work, either.

Do those in hell know what is happening to their loved ones? There's no indication here that they do. The rich man just knew his family. They probably hadn't changed much in the days he'd been gone. They, too, were on a highway to hell.

Can a dead man come to life and convince people to repent and give their lives to God? One did. His name is Jesus Christ. This dead man not only walked . . . He talked and appeared in the flesh. If that doesn't work to convince people about the reality of heaven, what will?

LUKE 23:42–43

And he said, "Jesus, remember me when you come into your kingdom." And he said to him, "Truly, I say to you, today you will be with me in Paradise." (ESV)

This is the Bible's best deathbed conversion.

With only moments to go before he died, the thief on the cross turned to Jesus and asked for mercy. He called out while dying, "Remember me," and Jesus responded, "Yes, I will remember."

Jesus said that the thief, the guilty one accused of crimes on earth, would be not guilty in heaven and would be free of his sins "today." Right now! God's forgiveness process does not get bogged down in red tape. It's immediate. And that's good news for people about to die.

With just a simple request—crying out to God for help—the Bible promises instant forgiveness and an invitation into paradise.

Jesus will not forget you as long as you ask to be remembered.

JOHN 5:28–29

"Do not marvel at this, for an hour is coming when all who are in the tombs will hear his voice and come out, those who have done good to the resurrection of life, and those who have done evil to the resurrection of judgment." (ESV)

All will hear.
All will rise.
The good—those who followed the true good (not the worldly good) in Christ Jesus—will rise and be alive.

The evil—those who followed the god of this world and pursued selfish interests (that they thought were good)—will rise and be sentenced to death apart from God.

The good leave behind the graves, where death exists. They will never see death again.

The evil exit their earthly graves but enter a new place, an eternal grave where they experience the feelings and emotions of death and separation all the time.

We will all hear and we will all rise. Some of us will be commended while others will be condemned.

JOHN 6:27

"Do not work for the food that perishes, but for the food that endures to eternal life, which the Son of Man will give to you. For on him God the Father has set his seal." (ESV)

We work to feed our mouths, which satisfies us temporarily. We should work to feed our souls, which satisfies us eternally.

What is the food that endures to eternity? Salvation, which the Son of Man gives us. Salvation through His Word and the work of Christ on the cross.

Now that we have that food, what work do we do in response?

Please God. Spread the good news. Serve our church. Love our neighbors. Love our enemies. Submit to others. Be examples in our marriages. Be examples in our schools and at work. Do good to all people.

That work achieves something greater than a paycheck that we spend at the grocery store for a cart full of food. This work feeds people's souls forever.

JOHN 14:2-4

"My Father's house has many rooms; if that were not so, would I have told you that I am going there to prepare a place for you? And if I go and prepare a place for you, I will come back and take you to be with me that you also may be where I am. You know the way to the place where I am going."

Jesus portrays himself in this verse as the builder, servant, and concierge of the greatest hotel ever built.

It has plenty of rooms, built to hold every believer who ever lived.

Like a servant, Jesus is getting our rooms ready, adding those last-minute touches.

When the time comes to check in, He wants to escort us to our rooms and welcome us there.

Once we are in our place, there is no checkout time. We don't have to be out by noon and there are no extra charges, no hidden costs. Jesus paid the bill.

Jesus just wants us to feel welcomed. He wants us to come and be with Him where He is.

And we all know where to find Him—in this heavenly hotel that we will soon call home.

ACTS 2:24

> But God raised him from the dead, freeing him from the
> agony of death, because it was impossible for death to keep
> its hold on him.

It's impossible for death to keep a good man down.

Death tried to stop Jesus, but He had power over the grave.

Our scientists and doctors do a good job fending off death and keeping it at bay, though they are only successful at adding a few years to life.

Death always wins.

Except in one case.

Because Jesus demonstrated His power over the grave, He promised to share the benefits of that power with us. We all get a resurrection date.

Sound impossible? Not for Jesus.

Nothing is impossible for Him.

ACTS 7:55–56

But he [Stephen], being full of the Holy Spirit, gazed into heaven and saw the glory of God, and Jesus standing at the right hand of God, and said, "Look! I see the heavens opened and the Son of Man standing at the right hand of God!" (NKJV)

Stephen, moments before his brutal death, got a sneak peek into his final destination.

The coming attraction revealed heaven and Jesus Christ standing with God the Father.

This was all Stephen needed to fill him with joy at his most desperate moment.

Despite his world falling apart, Stephen saw that Jesus was standing right where He promised He would be, and God was still on His throne.

Even though everything had turned upside down on earth, God still reigned in heaven. God was in His place and knew what was going on in Stephen's life.

Stephen's vision was for his persecutors, too, to make them wonder what they would see someday: the welcoming arms of Jesus Christ, or an accusing finger pointing them to depart because God never knew them.

ROMANS 2:16

> This will take place on the day when God judges people's
> secrets through Jesus Christ, as my gospel declares.

God will judge our secrets on Judgment Day.
So you must ask yourself, "What am I secretly hiding or planning? What secret motivations drive me and guide my day?"

Jesus Christ had no secrets. He lived a life of transparency. We should do the same. At our funeral, we don't want those secrets to come out. We don't want hidden boxes discovered in our garages or disappointing files on our computers.

With God there are no secrets. We think our secrets are hidden, but not to Him.

God will judge us by those secrets as well as our actions.

Stop hiding secrets in the dark and start revealing them in the light—the light of God—before someone else finds them when you die.

ROMANS 8:18

For I consider that the sufferings of this present time are not worthy to be compared with the glory which shall be revealed in us. (NKJV)

Whatever you're going through now will be like a hiccup you had ten years ago. Remember that hiccup? Of course you don't. That's how traumatic these moments will be when compared to the day you enter God's glory.

You don't even think about that time you had a stomachache fifteen years ago. It felt bad at the time, but it came and went with hardly a second thought.

You could be enduring a horrible disease right now, but when you enter heaven—healed and in the presence of Jesus Christ—it will be like that time you stubbed your toe twenty years ago.

Present sufferings will be stuffed so far in the past that they will be forgotten, because our minds will be so totally focused on the joy of being in the presence of God's glory and the eternal future that awaits us.

1 CORINTHIANS 15:42–44

So also is the resurrection of the dead. The body is sown in
corruption, it is raised in incorruption. It is sown in dishonor,
it is raised in glory. It is sown in weakness, it is raised in
power. It is sown a natural body, it is raised a spiritual body.
There is a natural body, and there is a spiritual body. (NKJV)

When we die, our bodies will be sown in the ground
like seeds.
Those bodies will enter the ground, proving how
fragile life was all along, but resurrect one day into a body that
will be indestructible.

Our bodies will die with a track record of sin, but raised in
righteousness . . . those sins all forgiven.

Our bodies will be put in the ground as proof to our weak-
nesses, but they will be raised to be with God on high.

Our bodies will naturally turn to dust but be raised super-
naturally whole, with a brand-new physical/spiritual body that
God designed for us.

Death is like a single seed that will eventually grow into a
bountiful harvest.

1 CORINTHIANS 15:55

"Where, O death, is your victory?
Where, O death, is your sting?"

Paul gives a shout-out to Hosea 13:14.
But now, with a New Testament point of view, it's almost said with a sarcastic snicker at Death.

"You thought you were soooo tough, Death. You thought nothing could stop you. You went around hurting people and making them fear you. You were so wrong, Death. You have met your match in Jesus Christ! Take that, Death! *Boom!*"

Death ain't got nuthin' on those who believe.

It's not as tough as it thinks it is.

2 CORINTHIANS 5:1

For we know that if our earthly house, this tent, is destroyed, we have a building from God, a house not made with hands, eternal in the heavens. (NKJV)

A tent or a house? Which do you prefer?

Tents are nice if you want to get outdoors and back to nature, but they cannot stand up to the brutal, blistering elements of rain, wind, or cold.

Buildings can withstand just about anything—solid and secure with stone foundations and layers of reinforcements.

God promises us an eternal building constructed and designed by Him, not humans. This body will never fall apart and has an eternal warranty.

We must never forget that our earthly bodies were not made to last forever, but our resurrected bodies will be. When we move into those new bodies, we'll see how much more glorious was the upgrade and never long for those tent-filled days again.

When you die, your body gets an upgrade and you'll never look back.

2 CORINTHIANS 5:6

Therefore we are always confident and know that as long
as we are at home in the body we are away from the Lord.

Most of us like our current home. The body has become
a comfortable place to live.
However, our real home is with the Lord.
We are anxious to get there, too.

While we wait, we can have confidence. We don't have to wonder if we are going to heaven. God wants us to know right now.

If we know, then we can have peace. No worries. No panic
attacks. No pressure. No rush.

We have a permanent address in heaven and a temporary
address on earth.

That day when we change our address will be the best move
we've ever made.

PHILIPPIANS 1:23–24

I am torn between the two: I desire to depart and be with Christ, which is better by far; but it is more necessary for you that I remain in the body.

W e are certainly torn between *better* and *necessary*. We want to be with God—which is better—but we want to stay here on earth for others—which feels necessary right now.

There is so much to do here before we leave. We must love and take care of our families. Encourage those who are hurting. Witness to those who are lost. Provide for those who are poor. Necessary things.

When God determines that our time is over, He will call us to a better home, and hopefully our lives here will have left an impact.

So what's better and what's necessary? Better will always be there, in heaven with God. Necessary is what we need to do now, here on earth.

We must do what is necessary now so the better will be even better when we get to heaven.

PHILIPPIANS 3:10–11

That I may know Him and the power of His resurrection
and the fellowship of His sufferings, being conformed to His
death; in order that I may attain to the resurrection from
the dead. (NASB)

To know Christ means . . .
     to know power.
     to know resurrection.
to know suffering.
to know death.
Is there anything else on this earth that we absolutely need
to know?

God sent His Son to the earth to overpower death and give
all believers eternal life so they can be resurrected like Him
from the dead.

What other knowledge will ever really matter when you face
death?

PHILIPPIANS 3:13–14

Brethren, I do not regard myself as having laid hold of it yet;
but one thing I do: forgetting what lies behind and reaching
forward to what lies ahead, I press on toward the goal for
the prize of the upward call of God in Christ Jesus. (NASB)

No runner has ever won a race by facing backwards.
A runner never even looks back because it slows
down his progression forward to the finish line, where
a prize awaits.

Christians must be more like runners. We must forget the
past and focus on the future. Will it be a strain? Yes, but God
tells us to press on.

What are we pressing on toward? The prize.

Where is that prize? In heaven. God, our biggest cheerleader,
calls us toward it.

"Keep running! You're almost there! Faster!"

What is that prize? Eternal life with Jesus Christ in heaven,
and hearing God yell as we cross the finish line, "Well done,
good and faithful servant!"

1 THESSALONIANS 4:13

Brothers and sisters, we do not want you to be uninformed about those who sleep in death, so that you do not grieve like the rest of mankind, who have no hope.

Grief and hope are not contradictions. You can do both at the same time.

Grief mourns the loss of someone on earth. Hope knows they are in heaven.

Grief weeps for the missing moments not spent with someone on earth. Hope looks forward to the time that will be spent with loved ones in heaven.

Grief cannot process how life will be on earth without our loved one. Hope is assured their life in heaven will be far better.

Grief is earthly. Hope is heavenly. We grieve on earth, but we hope toward heaven.

As time passes, our grief subsides and our hope increases, all the more as our own eternal day approaches. We will not grieve our own deaths. We will experience the full realization of our hope.

1 THESSALONIANS 4:14

For if we believe that Jesus died and rose again, even so God will bring with Him those who have fallen asleep in Jesus. (NASB)

F allen asleep" means the state of a deceased body at rest. The soul is awake, but the body sleeps peacefully in the grave.

Then the alarm clock for eternity goes off. God wakes those sleeping bodies to eternal activity. What happened to Jesus with His resurrection from the grave will happen to us.

Our physical bodies will rest—but not for long. They will be reunited with our spirits, which have been awake the entire time.

No hitting the Snooze button that day.

We normally don't like alarm clocks, but that sound at the resurrection we will love: our last wake-up call as body and soul reunite.

1 THESSALONIANS 4:16–18

For the Lord Himself will descend from heaven with a shout, with the voice of the archangel and with the trumpet of God, and the dead in Christ will rise first. Then we who are alive and remain will be caught up together with them in the clouds to meet the Lord in the air, and so we shall always be with the Lord. Therefore comfort one another with these words. (NASB)

C an you imagine this moment? Resurrection Day. The second coming of Christ.

The Lord himself coming down from heaven . . .
The voice of the archangel shouts . . .
Trumpets blast . . .
The dead who believed in Christ rise first . . .
Then any of those still alive will be caught up into heaven . . .
And all those who put their faith in Christ will be with Him forever.

What hopeful words these are no matter what situation you are presently going through. There's an incredible day coming that will make us forget about all the good and bad moments of our lives.

Be encouraged and comforted as you think about this great day that will soon come.

2 TIMOTHY 4:7–8

I have fought the good fight, I have finished the race, I have kept the faith. Henceforth there is laid up for me the crown of righteousness, which the Lord, the righteous judge, will award to me on that Day, and not only to me but also to all who have loved his appearing. (ESV)

After every boxing match and every race, there is an awards ceremony. Somebody has to win in order to make it an official competition.

The believer also has to fight against the naysayers, the skeptics, the bullies, the discouragers, the diseases, the sins of this world.

The believer also has to outrun the setbacks, the aches and pains, the failures, the temptations of this world.

At the finish line, they receive a crown of righteousness, but not because of what they did. They may have won some battles, but in reality they lost the war to sin.

The crown of righteousness is awarded to believers because Jesus won every boxing match and finished first in every race.

It's His crown He allows us to wear. It's His victory we celebrate when we cross the finish line.

HEBREWS 4:13

Nothing in all creation is hidden from God's sight. Everything is uncovered and laid bare before the eyes of him to whom we must give account.

W e have to stand before God and give an account for everything we ever did. And we can't lie; He already knows.

The best response is just to confess it all.

We all will die and be judged. Nobody gets a free pass.

The best thing to know is that once we confess it all, God will forgive it all because Jesus paid it all.

In fact, it's better to confess it all right now and get it out of the way. It'll be good practice for Judgment Day.

HEBREWS 11:16

But as it is, they desire a better country, that is, a heavenly one. Therefore God is not ashamed to be called their God, for he has prepared for them a city. (ESV)

A re you a country person or a city person? Do you think more nationally or locally? Are you a big-picture thinker or more focused on one place?

Good news. Heaven is both a country and a city.

It's a country because it will have its own king and sovereign authority.

It's also like a bustling city full of activity, with people interacting and relating to one another.

Both of these definitions describe heaven—authority and relationship—where God is King and we are His people. It's a place unlike any on earth.

This city/country is being prepared to meet all our needs, no matter which you prefer. It will be our home forever—a city bigger than any country in history, a country more intimate and relatable than any small village you can find on the map.

81

JAMES 4:14–15

Yet you do not know what tomorrow will bring. What is
your life? For you are a mist that appears for a little time and
then vanishes. Instead you ought to say, "If the Lord wills,
we will live and do this or that." (ESV)

We have no idea what will happen. We may not die
tomorrow, but one day that "tomorrow" will be the
day we die.

Life is short, especially in light of eternity. Our lives are just
blips on the screen, a mist in the air, a blink of the eye.

This verse from James tells us that instead of fighting for
more life, we should fight for more of God's will.

What difference does another year of blippin' life mean?
Another misty month? Even a blinkin' day?

We should be content only with living the life that coincides
with God's will.

His will has eternal ramifications. My will is only a preoc-
cupation with today or tomorrow.

Live a life that matters for many, many, many tomorrows . . .
according to God's will.

1 JOHN 5:11

And this is the testimony, that God gave us eternal life, and this life is in his Son. (ESV)

We are given eternal life. It's a gift.
But eternal life isn't a package deal or a pass to a holiday forever.

Eternal life is a relationship. If you love God's Son, you get the life.

Jesus is the entire package deal.

If you want to hang out with Jesus at church, then He'll be your Sunday friend.

If you want to hang out with Jesus forever, then He's your eternal King.

When you truly believe in Him and what He did for you, He'll invite you to stay over, not just for the night, but for eternity.

With Jesus you get it all—the relationship and the life.

REVELATION 3:5

The one who is victorious will, like them, be dressed in white. I will never blot out the name of that person from the book of life, but will acknowledge that name before my Father and his angels.

They keep records in heaven. In a book.

You want your name to appear in this book. It's called the Book of Life.

Once your name is written in the Book, it's there forever. No eraser can erase. Time cannot wear the page down.

There will come a time when Jesus looks over those records and acknowledges the ones who He approves to get in.

Imagine Jesus acknowledging your name as He scans the Book. "Yes, here it is. We have a place reserved for you. Step this way."

That's a list you don't want to miss.

Is your name in the Book?

REVELATION 4:8

The four living creatures, each having six wings, were full of
eyes around and within. And they do not rest day or night,
saying:
"Holy, holy, holy,
Lord God Almighty,
Who was and is and is to come!" (NKJV)

E very creature and angel in heaven cannot help themselves.
They must praise God!
But why? They've seen Him for such a long time.
What about Him haven't they noticed before? What surprises
them and causes them to cry out with praise over and over?

It's God's holiness. His righteousness and purity is so amazing that even the angels who have seen God forever can't stop
crying out.

"He's holy! So holy! So amazingly holy! Look how holy He
is! Have you ever seen such holiness!"

We, too, will not grow tired of His holiness. We will be join-
ing the chorus and every moment be amazed by God.

REVELATION 4:9–10

Whenever the living creatures give glory and honor and thanks to Him who sits on the throne, who lives forever and ever, the twenty-four elders fall down before Him who sits on the throne and worship Him who lives forever and ever, and cast their crowns before the throne. (NKJV)

There will be a time when Academy Award winners will drop their Oscars at the feet of God.

National champions in sports will take off their rings.

Business executives will throw down their portfolios.

Pastors will surrender their reserved parking spaces.

All of the earthly crowns of accomplishments we received will seem like nothing when we see God. Instead of ourselves receiving all glory, honor, and thanks for what we did, we'll turn it around and give God all the glory, honor, and thanks.

No longer will we be national champs, gold medal winners, and employees of the month. We will surrender it all to the King of Kings.

REVELATION 7:16–17

"Never again will they hunger;
never again will they thirst.
The sun will not beat down on them,"
nor any scorching heat.
For the Lamb at the center of the throne
will be their shepherd;
"he will lead them to springs of living water."
"And God will wipe away every tear from their eyes."

L et this verse sink in for a moment.
In heaven there is no more hunger.
No more thirst.
No more scorching heat.
No more death.
No more tears.

Why? Because Jesus is sitting right there as our King and Shepherd.

He is in control (King), and He is taking care of us (Shepherd).

Never again will we face the pain of this world.

The Shepherd King is in charge.

REVELATION 20:11

Then I saw a great white throne and Him who sat on it, from whose face the earth and the heaven fled away. And there was found no place for them. (NKJV)

Only one person can sit on a great white throne.

He must be great, awesome in might.

He must be pure, holy, and righteous.

He must have power, the ultimate authority over all things.

Every decision begins and ends with Him on the throne. Nothing has its being without approval from the great white throne.

This awesome, holy, authoritative leader commands so much power, He can remove the existing earth and the heavens with just a look.

This is who we get to worship for eternity. Why not start now?

REVELATION 20:12

And I saw the dead, small and great, standing before God, and books were opened. And another book was opened, which is the Book of Life. And the dead were judged according to their works, by the things which were written in the books. (NKJV)

Two sets of books in heaven.

One appears to have all the sinful charges accumulated by the dead during their lifetime.

The other book lists all those forgiven of those sinful charges.

One book lists all who must plead guilty and be charged.

The other book lists all who pleaded guilty and were already forgiven of any charges.

One book contains the names of those who thought the "good" of their lives would get them off the hook.

The other book contains the names of those who knew that only the righteousness of Christ could allow them the privilege to be forgiven.

Your name will be in one book or the other. Which one will it be?

REVELATION 20:13

And the sea gave up the dead which were in it, and death and Hades gave up the dead which were in them; and they were judged, every one of them according to their deeds. (NASB)

On that day of resurrection, all those who perished in the sea will rise up. All those buried in the ground will come forth.

This is not *Night of the Living Dead*. This is the Day of the Living God!

At the resurrection, we return to those eternal bodies we were always meant to have and immediately face a court date. No, not jury duty. We will be the ones on trial, standing before God in judgment.

Those resurrected bodies will then go to their eternal resting place. If our sin was paid for by Jesus Christ, we are set free, escorted to be with God. If our sin is unforgiven, we are guilty as charged and removed from the presence of God to life in prison.

It will be either the best day or the worst day of our lives.

You can make sure it's the best day right now and plead guilty to God.

REVELATION 20:14–15

> Then death and Hades were thrown into the lake of fire. This is the second death, the lake of fire. And if anyone's name was not found written in the book of life, he was thrown into the lake of fire. (NASB)

The lake of fire will be the eternal resting place of all things no longer associated with God. This place will be known as a second death.

The first death is when we die and are placed into the grave. That death occurs on earth.

Then, after Judgment Day, there will come a time when Death will be put to death. Hades, the grave, will no longer be needed. They will be tossed into the lake of fire.

Also thrown in will be those who refused God before their first death and now will be put away forever from God. They will "die" to God and be removed from the giver of life. For them, this is a second death. They will be sent to the lake of fire, where all hopes, all dreams, all freedom, and all possibilities of love are nothing more than ashes in a furnace.

One day, death will die and God will forever separate himself from anything that opposes His life.

REVELATION 21:1

Then I saw a new heaven and a new earth; for the first heaven
and the first earth passed away. . . . (NASB)

We like new things. New clothes. That new-car smell. A new attitude. A new job. New things bring the promise of starting fresh with new opportunities.

A new heaven and a new earth. Imagine that.

This earth we have here is pretty good, breathtaking and beautiful, but the new one will be much better. The heavens we see are massive and awe-inspiring, but in the new heaven, we will have God to stare at instead.

The new heaven and new earth will never grow old to us. They will always have that new-earth smell.

REVELATION 21:4

"He will wipe every tear from their eyes. There will be no
more death or mourning or crying or pain, for the old order
of things has passed away."

The old order of things was pain caused by separation—
being separated from a loved one, being separated from
health, being separated from goodness.

The new order of things becomes all about reconciliation
and a permanent relationship with God. No longer will we cry
because of death or illness or our poor choices that led to sin.
We will be reunited with life, healing, and forgiveness.

Never again will we see a tissue or need a hankie.

The only tears we will experience will be wept for joy.

REVELATION 21:22

I did not see a temple in the city, because the Lord God Almighty and the Lamb are its temple.

Everything that happened in the earthly temple pointed to the experience of heaven.

In the Bible, the temple represented the place where God lived and where you went to connect with God and take care of your sin. Sacrifices and prayers occurred there so you could reconcile with God and fulfill the requirements of the law.

In heaven, there is no need for the temple. God is the temple.

We don't have to go to a place to meet God. We are with God face-to-face.

We don't have to reconcile with God. We are His sons and daughters.

We don't have to seek forgiveness for our sins. Our sins have been forgiven and the slate wiped clean.

Technically the temple on earth does not go away in heaven. It just becomes a person, what it was intended to represent all along.

REVELATION 21:23–24

And the city has no need of sun or moon to shine on it, for
the glory of God gives it light, and its lamp is the Lamb. By
its light will the nations walk, and the kings of the earth will
bring their glory into it. (ESV)

God is literally the light of eternity.
We don't need to turn on lamps or buy flashlights.
We won't need candles or torches to find our way. God
provides permanent illumination in heaven.

No more Daylight Saving Time. We don't need to save time.
We have all the time we need.

No more worry in the darkness about thieves or robbers. All
evil is gone and all bad intentions with it.

We won't have to pay the power bill, because Jesus paid it
all by dying for us to save us from darkness and bring us into
the light.

The lights will always be on and you'll always be home.

REVELATION 21:25–26

On no day will its gates ever be shut, for there will be no night there. The glory and honor of the nations will be brought into it.

The gates of heaven never need to be shut. There is no enemy to be protected from.

We won't need walls to keep out enemy nations. All nations will be represented there, living in peace.

We will experience the security of walls and gates, providing boundaries that we enjoy in our lives now, yet in heaven, God will be our security. The walls only remind us who really is our strength and our fortress.

The open gates seem to express a freedom to explore—maybe the new heavens and the new earth? Hopefully we can travel back and forth and praise God for His wonderful creation. Heaven becomes an adventure!

Wherever we go, we will be one nation with one leader and one purpose—to love God and one another.

REVELATION 21:27

Nothing impure will ever enter it, nor will anyone who does
what is shameful or deceitful, but only those whose names
are written in the Lamb's book of life.

We live in a world of trash and pollution. We've grown used to the mess and shrug it off as "life." Dirt is the norm.

The same is true for sin. Sin seems shocking at first, but over time it starts to grow on you. Next thing you know, sin has moved in and made its home.

Sin is not welcome in heaven. For the first time ever, we will step into a place where there is nothing dirty, impure, shameful, or deceitful. Everything—the people, the surroundings, and God himself—will be pure, righteous, and holy.

It will be shocking to us—like breathing clear, fresh air for the first time—but it will feel right. We will have wondered how we lived life before in such filth and immediately rejoice in this new and wonderful environment.

REVELATION 22:3

No longer will there be any curse. The throne of God and of the Lamb will be in the city, and his servants will serve him.

We will serve God in heaven.

Interesting thought, which brings up the question . . . What will we do?

We can certainly serve God in worship, but will that be all?

Hopefully we can serve God by serving others in heaven. Maybe some can use their gifts of speaking to tell stories about God. Some could act out dramas or write soliloquies or songs of praise.

Others could cook the great banquets and serve their guests; some could work in the fields and harvest the fruit.

We will serve wholeheartedly, without worrying about how others see us. No job will be too great or too menial. We will all be servants receiving the same pay—the presence of God in heaven.

REVELATION 22:4–5

They will see his face, and his name will be on their foreheads.
And night will be no more. They will need no light of lamp
or sun, for the Lord God will be their light, and they will
reign forever and ever. (ESV)

The face of God cannot be accurately described in just a few earthly words right now.

We'll leave that to our imaginations until it becomes a reality.

We do know some things by what Scripture says about the face of God.

His face will shine radiantly.

His face will cause us to tremble. If we saw His face while we're alive on earth, the sight of it would cause us to die. When we are in heaven and unable to die, God's face will shake us to our soul.

His face will never grow old. We will constantly seek it, sneaking a peek at it, gazing at it, and ultimately resting in it.

His face will mean to us that He is right there with us, watching over us, and we will have nothing to fear ever again.

REVELATION 22:12

"Look, I am coming soon! My reward is with me, and I will give to each person according to what they have done."

Soon.

Jesus is coming for us sooner than we think.

And He's bringing rewards.

If we've done good and looked to Jesus Christ for our righteousness, we will get a good gift—adoption into the Eternal Kingdom to live with God.

If someone's done bad and looked to himself or herself for self-righteousness, there's a reward for that, too. He'll get to be by himself forever.

Are you looking forward to that tea at three or that vacation in two weeks or a wedding in six months. . . ? Or are you looking forward to, anticipating, rejoicing in the return of Jesus Christ to earth?

It will happen sooner rather than later. Are you ready for that day?

REVELATION 22:17

And the Spirit and the bride say, "Come!" And let him who hears say, "Come!" And let him who thirsts come. Whoever desires, let him take the water of life freely. (NKJV)

An eternal relationship in heaven with God through Jesus Christ is an open invitation.

Just come.

Especially those who are thirsty. You know you thirst for something, and you've tried to fill it with the drinks of the world—unhealthy relationships, destructive habits, and ungodly sins. It hasn't quenched your thirst, or you've woken up with a hangover of guilt.

Come drink the water of life. Recognize that you are sinful, and one sip of God's drink will clean you up. You'll taste the love of Jesus Christ and experience His forgiveness. Gone will be all the tears, shame, and pain.

It's a free gift for us that cost Jesus Christ everything.

You won't regret drinking this drink. In fact, you'll be sipping on it in heaven forever.

SCRIPTURE LIST

1. Genesis 3:19
2. Genesis 3:22
3. Genesis 5:24
4. Genesis 25:8
5. Genesis 28:12
6. Exodus 12:13
7. Exodus 15:13
8. Exodus 33:19–20
9. 2 Samuel 12:22–23
10. Esther 4:16
11. Job 1:21
12. Job 13:15
13. Job 14:5
14. Job 19:25–27
15. Job 33:28
16. Psalm 14:2
17. Psalm 16:9–10
18. Psalm 18:4–6
19. Psalm 23:4
20. Psalm 23:6
21. Psalm 27:4
22. Psalm 39:4–5
23. Psalm 44:25–26
24. Psalm 49:15
25. Psalm 49:16–17
26. Psalm 62:1–2
27. Psalm 68:20
28. Psalm 73:25
29. Psalm 73:26
30. Psalm 84:10
31. Psalm 89:47–48
32. Psalm 90:12
33. Psalm 100:4
34. Psalm 103:14–16
35. Psalm 116:3–4
36. Psalm 139:16
37. Ecclesiastes 3:1–2
38. Ecclesiastes 3:19–20
39. Isaiah 6:5
40. Isaiah 11:6
41. Isaiah 38:5
42. Isaiah 43:25

43. Isaiah 65:17
44. Daniel 6:26–27
45. Hosea 13:14
46. Jonah 2:6
47. Matthew 6:19–21
48. Matthew 12:36–37
49. Matthew 13:41–43
50. Matthew 19:28–30
51. Matthew 22:30
52. Matthew 25:21
53. Matthew 25:31–32
54. Matthew 25:34
55. Matthew 25:46
56. Mark 12:27
57. Luke 16:22–23
58. Luke 16:26
59. Luke 16:27–28
60. Luke 23:42–43
61. John 5:28–29
62. John 6:27
63. John 14:2–4
64. Acts 2:24
65. Acts 7:55–56
66. Romans 2:16
67. Romans 8:18
68. 1 Corinthians 15:42–44
69. 1 Corinthians 15:55
70. 2 Corinthians 5:1
71. 2 Corinthians 5:6

72. Philippians 1:23–24
73. Philippians 3:10–11
74. Philippians 3:13–14
75. 1 Thessalonians 4:13
76. 1 Thessalonians 4:14
77. 1 Thessalonians 4:16–18
78. 2 Timothy 4:7–8
79. Hebrews 4:13
80. Hebrews 11:16
81. James 4:14–15
82. 1 John 5:11
83. Revelation 3:5
84. Revelation 4:8
85. Revelation 4:9–10
86. Revelation 7:16–17
87. Revelation 20:11
88. Revelation 20:12
89. Revelation 20:13
90. Revelation 20:14–15
91. Revelation 21:1
92. Revelation 21:4
93. Revelation 21:22
94. Revelation 21:23–24
95. Revelation 21:25–26
96. Revelation 21:27
97. Revelation 22:3
98. Revelation 22:4–5
99. Revelation 22:12
100. Revelation 22:17

TROY SCHMIDT is an author and television writer with credits at Disney, Nickelodeon, Tommy Nelson, and Lifeway. He has written for Max Lucado's HERMIE AND FRIENDS series and was the consulting producer for *The American Bible Challenge* with Jeff Foxworthy. His other book titles include *Saved, Release, 40 Days, Chapter by Chapter, In His Shoes: The Life of Jesus,* and many others. Troy has also written several children's books, including *Little Tree Found* and *Their Side of the Story.* He is a campus pastor at First Baptist Church of Windemere, Florida. Troy and his wife have three grown sons and make their home in Florida.

Let God's Word Show You How to Have a Richer Prayer Life

Countless books have been written about how to pray, what to pray, and when to pray. But wouldn't it be great if God himself gave us these answers? In fact, He already has! Using 100 key verses from Scripture, this book will answer such questions as:

- How do I know God hears my prayers?
- What should I ask Him when I pray?
- How can I worship and praise God through prayer?
- How should I pray for those I love?

Like *The 100 Best Bible Verses on Heaven,* this book includes well-known gems and hidden treasures that will surprise you. Each verse is followed by a brief reading to explain the verse's significance and draw you closer to God in prayer.

The 100 Best Bible Verses on Prayer by Troy Schmidt

◊ BETHANYHOUSE

Stay up-to-date on your favorite books and authors with our free e-newsletters. Sign up today at bethanyhouse.com.

Find us on Facebook. facebook.com/BHPnonfiction

Follow us on Twitter. @bethany_house